The Development of Blockchain Technology

T0255972

Center for Electronics and Information Studies,
Chinese Academy of Engineering

The Development of Blockchain Technology

Research on the Development of Electronic
Information Engineering Technology in China

Science Press
Beijing

Springer

Center for Electronics and Information Studies, Chinese Academy of Engineering
Beijing, China

ISBN 978-981-16-7235-4   ISBN 978-981-16-7236-1   (eBook)
https://doi.org/10.1007/978-981-16-7236-1

Jointly published with Science Press
The print edition is not for sale in China (Mainland). Customers from China (Mainland) please order the
print book from Science Press.

This Springer imprint is published by the registered company Springer Nature Singapore Pte Ltd.
The registered company address is: 152 Beach Road, #21-01/04 Gateway East, Singapore 189721,
Singapore

Preface

The "Research on the Development of Electronic Information Engineering Technology in China" book series

In today's world, the wave of information technologies featured by digitalization, networking, and intelligence is gaining momentum. Information technologies are experiencing rapid changes with each passing day and are fully applied in production and life, bringing about profound changes in global economic, political, and security landscapes. Among diverse information technologies, electronic information engineering technology is one of the most innovative and widely used technologies and plays its greatest role in driving the development of other S&T fields. It is not only a field of intense competition in technological innovation, but also an important strategic direction for key players to fuel economic growth and seek competitive advantages over other players. Electronic information engineering technology is a typical "enabling technology" that enables technological progress in almost all other fields. Its integration with biotechnology, new energy technology, and new material technology is expected to set off a new round of technological revolution and industrial transformation, thereby bringing about new opportunities for the evolution of human society. Electronic information is a typical "engineering technology" and one of the most straightforward and practical tools. It realizes direct and close integration of scientific discoveries and technological innovations with industrial developments, greatly speeding up technological progress. Hence, it is regarded as a powerful force to change the world. Electronic information engineering technology is a vital driving force of China's rapid economic and social development in the past seven decades, especially in the past four decades of reform and opening up. Looking ahead, advances and innovations in electronic information engineering technology will remain to be one of the most important engines driving human progress.

CAE is China's foremost academic and advisory institution in engineering and technological sciences. Guided by the general development trends of science and technology around the world, CAE is committed to providing scientific, forward-looking, and timely advice for innovation-driven scientific and technological progress from a strategic and long-term perspective. CAE's mission is to function as a national high-end think tank. To fulfill the mission, the Division of Information and Electronics, under the guidance of its Vice President Zuoning Chen, Director Xicheng Lu, and the Standing Committee, mobilized more than 300 academicians and experts to jointly compile the General Section and the Special Themes of this book (hereinafter referred to as the "Blue Book"). The first stage of compilation was headed by Academicians Jiangxing Wu and Manqing Wu (from the end of 2015 to June 2018), and the second one was headed by Academicians Shaohua Yu and Jun Lu (since September 2018). The purposes of compiling the Blue Book are:

By analyzing technological progress and introducing major breakthroughs and marked achievements made in the electronic information field both at home and abroad each year, to provide reference for China's scientific and technical personnel to accurately grasp the development trend of the field and provide support for China's policymakers to formulate related development strategies.

The "Blue Book" is compiled according to the following principles:

1. **Ensure appropriate description of annual increment.** The field of electronic information engineering technology enjoys a broad coverage and high development speed. Thus, the General Section should ensure an appropriate description of the annual increment, which is about the recent progress, new characteristics, and new trends.
2. **Selection of hot points and highlight points.** China's technological development is still at a mixed stage where it needs to assume the role of follower, contender, and leader simultaneously. Hence, the Special Themes should seek to depict the developmental characteristics the industry focuses on, and should center on the "hot points" and "highlight points" along the development journey.
3. **Integration of General Section and Special Themes.** The program consists of two sections: The General Section and the Special Themes. The former adopts a macro perspective to discuss the global and Chinese development of electronic information engineering technology and its outlook; the latter provides detailed descriptions of hot points and highlight points in the 13 subfields.

Application System

8. Underwater acoustic engineering

13. Computer application

Acquiring Perception	**Computation and Control**	**Cyber Security**
3. Sensing	10. Control	6. Network and communication
5. Electromagnetic space	11. Cognition	7. Cybersecurity
	12. Computer systems and software	

Common Basis

1. Microelectronics and Optoelectronics   2. Optical engineering

4. Measurement, metrology and Instruments

9. Electromagnetic field and electromagnetic environment effect

Classification Diagrams of 13 Subfields of information and electronic engineering technology

The above graphic displays five categories and 13 sub-categories, or special themes that bear distinct granularity. However, every subfield is closely connected with each other in terms of technological correlations, which allows easier matching with their corresponding disciplines.

Currently, the compilation of the "Blue Book" is still at a trial stage where careless omissions are unavoidable. Hence, we welcome comments and corrections.

"The Development of Blockchain Technology" in "Research on the Development of Electronic Information Engineering Technology in China" Book Series

In October 2019, the general secretary of the Communist Party of China Xi Jinping presided over the eighteenth group study session of the CPC Central Committee Political Bureau, underscored the important role of blockchain technology in the new round of technological innovation and industrial transformation, urging more efforts to quicken development in the sector. Blockchain technology has the technical characteristics of difficult to tamper and full traceability. It has great potential of application in promoting data sharing, improving collaborative efficiency, reducing operating costs, optimizing business processes, and building a trusted system.

In recent years, the blockchain technology industry maintains a strong momentum of innovation and development. Under the promotion of national industrial policy, China's blockchain industry has developed rapidly, and blockchain technology and solutions are constantly innovating.

To comprehensively present the development status, policy environment, key application directions, and the future development of blockchain technology industry, the Center for Electronics and Information Studies has organized and written *The Development of Blockchain Technology*. It provides a reference to understand the progress of blockchain technology and industry, and how to make better use of blockchain technology.

The book is divided into six chapters. The first chapter introduces the concept, development process, and core value of blockchain. Chapter 2 focuses on the core technology and classification of blockchain technology. Chapter 3 summarizes the development situation of the global and Chinese blockchain industry, including the status quo of policy measures, standard construction, and application development. Chapters 4 and 5 summarize the main innovation points of blockchain technology, including its development in China. Finally, Chapter 6 prospects the future development of blockchain technology.

With only 12 years of history, blockchain technology has made great progress in technology and industrial applications. However, from a long-term perspective, blockchain technology is still at the early stage of development, and there are many difficulties and obstacles to be overcome in all aspects of development. We will continue to track and in-depth research on blockchain according to the global development of blockchain and the feedback of the industry. Meanwhile, we will timely update and release the latest research results.

Beijing, China   Center for Electronics and Information Studies,
                                                              Chinese Academy of Engineering

Contents

List of Series Contributors

The guidance group and working group of '**Research on the Development of Electronic Information Engineering Technology in China**' series are shown as below:

Guidance Group

Leader: Zuoning Chen, Xichen Lu
Member (In alphabetical order):
Aiguo Fei, Baoyan Duan, Binxing Fang, Bohu Li, Changxiang Shen, Cheng Wu, Chengjun Wang, Chun Chen, Desen Yang, Dianyuan Fang, Endong Wang, Guangjun Zhang, Guangnan Ni, Guofan Jin, Guojie Li, Hao Dai, Hequan Wu, Huilin Jiang, Huixing Gong, Jiangxing Wu, Jianping Wu, Jiaxiong Fang, Jie Chen, Jiubin Tan, Jun Lu, Lianghui Chen, Manqing Wu, Qinping Zhao, Qionghai Dai, Shanghe Liu, Shaohua Yu, Tianchu Li, Tianran Wang, Tianyou Chai, Wen Gao, Wenhua Ding, Yu Wei, Yuanliang Ma, Yueguang Lv, Yueming Li, Zejin Liu, Zhijie Chen, Zhonghan Deng, Zhongqi Gao, Zishen Zhao, Zuyan Xu

Working Group

Leader: Shaohua Yu, Jun Lu
Deputy Leader: Da An, Meimei Dang, Shouren Xu
Member (In alphabetical order):
Denian Shi, Dingyi Zhang, Fangfang Dai, Fei Dai, Fei Xing, Feng Zhou, Gang Qiao, Lan Zhou, Li Tao, Liang Chen, Lun Li, Mo Liu, Nan Meng, Peng Wang, Qiang Fu, Qingguo Wang, Rui Zhang, Shaohui Li, Wei He, Wei Xie, Xiangyang Ji, Xiaofeng Hu, Xingquan Zhang, Xiumei Shao, Yan Lu, Ying Wu, Yue Lu, Yunfeng Wei, Yuxiang Shu, Zheng Zheng, Zhigang Shang, Zhuang Liu

About the Author

The Chinese Academy of Engineering (CAE) is China's foremost academic and advisory institution in engineering and technological sciences, which has been enrolled in the first batch of pilot national high-end think tanks. As a national institution, CAE's missions are to study major strategic issues in economic and social development as well as in engineering technology progress, and to build itself into a S&T think tank having significant influences on decision-making of national strategic issues. In today's world, the wave of information technologies featured by digitalization, networking, and intelligence is gaining momentum. Information technologies are experiencing rapid changes with each passing day and are fully applied in production and life, bringing about profound changes in global economic, political, and security landscapes. Among diverse information technologies, electronic information engineering technology is one of the most innovative and widely used technologies and plays its greatest role in driving the development of other S&T fields. In order to better carry out strategic studies on electronic information engineering technology, promote innovation in relevant systems and mechanisms, and integrate superior resources, China Research Center for Electronics and Information Strategies (hereinafter referred to the "Center") was established in November 2015 by CAE in collaboration with Cyberspace Administration of China (CAC), the Ministry of Industry and Information Technology (MIIT), and China Electronics Technology Group Corporation (CETC).

The Center pursues high-level, open, and prospective development and is committed to conducting theoretical and application-oriented researches on cross-cutting, overarching, and strategically important hot topics concerning electronic information engineering technologies, and providing consultancy services for policy making by brainstorming ideas from CAE academicians and experts and scholars from national ministries and commissions, businesses, public institutions, universities, and research institutions. The Center's mission is to build a top-notch strategic think tank that provides scientific, forward-looking, and timely advice for national policy making in terms of electronic information engineering technology.

The main authors of *The Development of Blockchain Technology* are Kai Wei, Shaohua Yu, and Chen Kang.

Chapter 1
The Concept and Benefits of Blockchain

1 The Concept of Blockchain

Blockchain is a public data management technology, which is maintained by multiple parties in a "decentralized" way, and the data is stored consistently by the consensus mechanism to achieve data tamper-proof, and prevention of repudiation. Different from the traditional centralized data management modes, each computer in the blockchain network retains all historical information and has a complete data history. At the same time, all computers in the network have the right to verify each piece of information, and finally, according to the "voting" results (consensus mechanism), the majority can decide what to write in the information to update the data for the whole network.

Network participants independently record and verify each piece of information on a public database held and maintained by multiple parties. Each network participant is both a data recorder and a data verifier. The data can be reviewed and shared by everyone, which is difficult to tamper with and verifiable in terms of the credit. The discontinuous "voting" and "accounting" in the network are based on "blocks". Therefore, the public ledger is a chain composed of "ledger blocks", so it is called "blockchain".

Based on the above technical characteristics, the blockchain has changed the traditional center-based information verification modes, reduced the establishment cost of "credit", and promoted the Internet to change from information transmission to value transmission.

© The Author(s), under exclusive license to Springer Nature Singapore Pte Ltd. 2022
Center for Electronics and Information Studies, Chinese Academy of Engineering,
The Development of Blockchain Technology,
https://doi.org/10.1007/978-981-16-7236-1_1

2   The History of Blockchain

Based on the development processes, the concept of blockchain originated in 2008 and was first proposed by Satoshi Nakamoto in the *Bitcoin: A Peer-to-peer Electronic Cash System*. The following year, Satoshi Nakamoto released the Bitcoin-Qt/ Bitcoin Core and completed the first accounting. The Bitcoin system was officially put into operation, marking the transition of blockchain technology from theory to practical operation, which was the 1.0 phase of blockchain development.

In 2014, Ethereum proposed the blockchain-based smart contracts, which greatly expanded the programmability of blockchain. Users can write programs for smart contracts and deploy them on the blockchain, which would upgrade the blockchain from a "proprietary ledger" which was mainly used to record transactions and transfers to a "general ledger" that can record program calculated results. The blockchain entered the programmable era then, greatly improving the application potential of the blockchain, which marked the 2.0 phase of blockchain development.

In 2014, some large organizations also began to introduce the idea of blockchain into the reforms of IT systems, and the application paradigm that combined the blockchain with the real economy was springing up. By adding components such as access control, entrepreneurs and managers applied blockchain technology to supply chain management, judicial records, digital copyrights, food and drug traceability and other aspects. Here came the 3.0 phase of blockchain development.

At the end of December 2019, the Division of Information and Electronic Engineering of Chinese Academy of Engineering released ten major technological trends in the information field. The article 10 noted: "the blockchain technology is rapidly growing and the application scenarios are constantly enriched. Efforts are made to build a trusted system in a digital society and reshape the way of value transmission in human society. The development of new digital currencies based on blockchain will become a hot spot for major powers and will have an impact on the global financial system."

3   The Benefits of Blockchain

In October 2015, *the Economist* defined blockchain as a mechanism to reshape human trust in a mechanized way in *The Promise of the Blockchain: The Trust Machine*. Blockchain technology fulfills the openness, transparency, traceability and difficulty in tampering of information dissemination through computer mechanisms such as data organization algorithm, consensus mechanism and peer-to-peer (P2P) network, which can bring a transparent and credible data flow basis to network participants and inspire trust.

The blockchain-based trust is a new form of human trust-based cooperation and an evolution of institution-based trust in the digital ages. It reaches the widest range of trust and a lower-cost trust establishment mechanism. As professor Kevin

Werbach of the University of Pennsylvania said in his treatise on blockchain-based trust, "Providing all users with the most generalized trust (credit) service is the core value of blockchain."

The basis of blockchain-based trust lies in the independent accounting and verification process of all parties in an equal and decentralized network. Each participant independently records and verifies each transaction and contract on a public ledger held and maintained by multiple parties. With the consensus mechanism, every network participant may become an accountant (bookkeeper), while with the transaction verification mechanism, every network (full node) is an auditor. Therefore, the blockchain is a network of common accounting and auditing. The consensus mechanism ensures the randomness, dispersibility and unforgeability of accounting, while transaction confirming verification ensures the legality of accounting.

Therefore, the blockchain-based trust is also a kind of trust intermediary, which converts the trust between people into the trust between people and machines. Furthermore, blockchain converts abstract social institution-based trust rules into rules written in machine language and executed automatically.

For blockchain users, they can complete their trust in accounting and contract calculation with no needs to trust any members who specifically participate in the network ecology. As long as the blockchain system functions properly, illegal and invalid transactions cannot pass the consensus confirmation process of common accounting and global auditing, so there is no room for default or dishonesty. In general, the blockchain-based trust expands the scope of trust with creativity, reduces the cost of trust, and opens up new possibilities for global integration and cooperation in a wider range. In the future development, the blockchain-based trust and institution-based trust may complement each other to build a more universal and efficient global trust system.

Chapter 2
The Core Technologies and Classifications of Blockchain

Blockchain is an integrated and innovative application of various IT technologies, mainly involving subject theories and technologies of computer science, cryptography, distributed systems, P2P network, etc. With the continuous upgrading of blockchain technology, the core technical framework of blockchain gradually becomes clear.

Block chain data structure is to verify and store data, distributed node consensus algorithms are to generate and update data, P2P network is to broadcast and transmit data, cryptography is to ensure the security of data transmission and access. Therefore, as a decentralized distributed ledger, the blockchain system mainly involves five core technologies: ledger data structure, consensus algorithm, P2P network, cryptography and smart contract.

1   Core Technologies of Blockchain

Ledger Data Structure

The ledger data structure is a data structure that stores transactions that take place in a certain period of time in blocks and connect the blocks into chains in chronological order by cryptographic algorithms. This data structure in "blocks" is also how the "blockchain" technology gets its name.

The latter block contains the characteristic information of the previous block, so if you want to modify the data in one of the blocks, you need to modify all the subsequent blocks in the linked structure. However, with the block height increasing, the difficulty of modification is also increasing. Therefore, the linked data structure effectively improves the tamper-proof and anti-forgery capabilities of the data stored therein.

© The Author(s), under exclusive license to Springer Nature Singapore Pte Ltd. 2022
Center for Electronics and Information Studies, Chinese Academy of Engineering,
The Development of Blockchain Technology,
https://doi.org/10.1007/978-981-16-7236-1_2

Table 2.1 Comparisons of two models in the ledger

	Asset-based	Account-based
Modeling objects	Asset	Account
Data record	Asset ownership	Account operation
System Center	Status (transaction)	Event (operation)
Computing concentration	Client	Node
Dependency judgement	Easy to estimate dependency	Difficult to estimate dependency
Parallel	Easy	Hard
Account management	Hard to manage account metadata	Easy to manage account metadata
Suitable query scenarios	Easy to fetch transaction status	Easy to fetch account balance
Client	Complex	Easy
Examples	Bitcoin, R3 Corda	Ethereum, hyper ledger fabric

The ledger can be categorized as asset-based leger and account-based ledger according to the way data recorded at the ledger. The comparisons of asset-based leger and account-based ledger are shown in Table 2.1. Asset is the core of asset-based ledger, and the ownership of the asset will be recorded on the ledger. Besides, the ownership recorded is only an item of ledger. In the account-based model, account is the core of ledger and asset is the next item next to account. Compared with asset-based model, account-based data model is much easier to record and query information related to account. While asset-based data model can adapt for concurrent environment better. To achieve better performance and query account status timely, more and more blockchain platforms have moved towards a hybrid model which combines asset-based leger and account-based ledger.

As more transactions are recorded on the ledger, more storage are needed for blockchain systems. And scalability issues of blockchain storage and nodes are of importance and urgent to solve. There are two kinds of solutions for that as reducing storage burden of the single chain and realizing the scalability of the blockchain system. The former can be implemented by weakening the traceability of blockchain. For example, the archiving function reduces the storage amount by deleting some cold data. The latter can be implemented through multi-chain integration and cross-chain interoperability, like homogeneous multi-chain and heterogeneous multi-chain. Among solutions, the multi-chain coordination is a more popular development trend, which combines these two directions at the ledger layer.

Consensus Algorithms

In untrusted environments, consensus algorithms are used to maintain data consistency between nodes due to the unreliability of nodes themselves and the instability of communication between nodes, and even the information forged by them for malicious response. With consensus algorithms, the blockchain coordinates the behaviors and states of multiple nodes that do not trust each other, thus forming a reliable system in an untrusted environment.

A consensus algorithm is a system implementation based on node behavior assumption, governance model and node network size assumption. In essence, the characteristics of the services on the chain and the positioning of the roles of network nodes determine the choice of consensus algorithms. With the diversification of node participation roles and the subdivision of business interaction characteristics, different network assumptions and governance models have emerged. How to become a public blockchain project that can be truly realized is the common exploration direction? It has bred the differences of consensus algorithms in consensus order, consensus rounds, finality and node selection methods to form a trend of diversified development. The evolution of the blockchain consensus mechanism also confirms that fact.

In the early stage of blockchain development, the mainly blockchain networks are based on consensus algorithms of PoW (Proof of Work). Due to the waste of energy in PoW, the research on consensus algorithms based on PoS (Proof of Stake) has developed rapidly since 2017. Single consensus algorithms have proven their own limitations, such as low efficiency of PoW consensus and low decentralization degree of DPoS. Blockchain researchers have been trying to integrate two or more consensus algorithms and learn from each other to achieve better consensus characteristics. The new consensus algorithms, such as Algorand, DFINITY, and VBFT, are all hybrid consensus algorithms (as shown in Table 2.2).

Peer-to-Peer (P2P) Network

P2P (Peer-to-Peer) refers to the fact that each node in the network has the same status. Each node not only acts as a server to provide services for other nodes, but also enjoys services provided by other nodes. Resources and services in P2P network are scattered on all nodes. Information transmission and service implementation are directly carried out between nodes, which can avoid possible bottlenecks and highlight the scalability and robustness of the network without the intervention of intermediate links and servers.

Each node in the blockchain is a typical server network, and they are equal to each other, regardless of priority. With the P2P communication mechanism, fast synchronization of data between nodes nearby can be realized. At the same time, the ability of the whole blockchain to resist network attacks is improved.

Table 2.2 Comparison of mainstream consensus algorithms

	Number of malicious nodes that are tolerable	Finality	Networking complexity (O means the message complexity and N stands for the network size)	Examples
PoW	Less than 1/2	The algorithm does not provide finality	$O(N)$	Bitcoin
Tendermint	Less than 1/3	Implemented through BFT	$O(N^2)$	Cosmos
Algorand	Less than 1/3	Implemented through byzantine agreement	$O(N*\log N)$	Algorand
EOS DPoS	Less than 1/3	Implemented through BFT	$O(1)$	EOS
DFINITY	Less than 1/3	Weighted evaluation of several historical blocks	$O(N*\log N)$	DFINITY
VBFT	Less than 1/3	Implemented through BFT	$O(N*\log N)$	Ontology
PoW-DAG	Less than 1/2	The algorithm does not provide finality	$O(N)$	Conflux

Cryptography

Cryptography ensures that transaction information is difficult to tamper with and authentication is carried out for transaction initiators. At the same time, in the scenario of consortium blockchain, cryptography can bring an access mechanism to blockchain system, allowing nodes to complete authentication and mutual recognition. Cryptographic algorithms commonly used in general blockchain systems include the hash function and asymmetric cryptographic algorithm.

The hash function is a general term for a type of encryption algorithms and is a very basic and important technology in the information technology field. It generally has four characteristics in the application process:

Firstly, the hash function is unidirectional, that is, the output value can be easily obtained by calculating the input value through the hash function, but it is difficult for us to infer what the corresponding input value is according to the output value, just as a piece of glass is easily smashed, but it is difficult to put all the broken pieces together again to make a complete glass.

Secondly, the calculation time of the hash function is short. No matter how large the original data is, the calculation time with the hash function is generally acceptable.

Thirdly, the hash function is sensitively dependent on the input, that is, as long as the input value is slightly modified, the final output value will generally be very different.

Fourth, the output of the hash function is fixed in size. No matter how long the input value is, the hash function calculation will output a fixed length output.

By using the above technical characteristics, the hash function can lead to fast forward calculation, but it is difficult in reverse derivation, and because of the sensitive dependence on input value, the final output value is resistant to impact, so as to ensure that the output hash can replace the original input value and reduce the verification difficulty and transmission cost.

In the blockchain system, the hash function is generally applied in the process of transaction verification and block construction. For example, transaction verification. With the hash function, transaction information can be compressed into a fixed-length output, a data summary can be generated, reducing transmission costs, while ensuring the authenticity of the data, and improving the efficiency of transaction verification.

Asymmetric encryption refers to an encryption algorithm that uses different keys to encrypt and decrypt. The ciphertext obtained by encrypting the plaintext with one of the keys can only be decrypted by the corresponding other key. Although the two keys are mathematically related, if one of them is known, the other cannot be calculated. The key that can be made public is commonly called a public key, while the key kept by the user secretly is commonly called a private key.

In the blockchain network, each user has a unique pair of public and private keys. The public key, just like credit card numbers, can be made public, while the private key should be stored securely, just like the account password of the bank card. In short, in the blockchain, the person who controls the private key will get all the data in the account corresponding to the private key. The typical application scenario of asymmetric encryption in blockchain system is the signing and verification of the transaction. The transaction initiator signs the original transaction information with the private key and broadcasts the signed transaction and the public key. After receiving the transaction, each node can verify whether the transaction is legal with the public key. In this process, the transaction initiator does not need to expose the private key, so as to ensure confidentiality.

Smart Contract

A smart contract refers to a program deployed on the blockchain that can run automatically, which can automatically execute the predefined rules and terms, reduce the risk of human intervention, and improve the security and credibility of transaction execution. The execution environment of the smart contract is called the smart contract engine.

Table 2.3 Smart contract characteristics of some blockchain systems

Blockchain platform	Turing completeness	Developing language
Bitcoin	Incomplete	Bitcoin Script
Ethereum	Complete	Solidity
EOS	Complete	C++
Hyperledger Fabric	Complete	Go
Hyperledger Sawtooth	Complete	Python
R3 Corda	Complete	Kotlin/Java

According to Turing Completeness,[1] smart contracts can be classified into Turing-Complete smart contracts and Non-Turing-Complete smart contracts. Factors that may affect Turing completeness include loop or recursion being constrained, incapable arrays implementation or containing complex data structures. Turing complete smart contracts have considerable adaptability and can be used for complex business operations. Compared with Turing-Complete smart contracts, Non-Turing-Complete smart contracts are simple, more efficient, and secure despite of incapable of operating complex business logic. As there are more application scenarios for smart contracts and smart contracts are not only a key part of blockchain system, but also a new technology direction on blockchain. A variety of mature virtual machines and interpreters have been introduced into smart contract applications, such as JVM and Python. Characteristics of smart contracts of blockchain systems are shown in the Table 2.3.

Security of smart contracts is important to security of blockchain systems. In recent years, there are many security incidents which are caused by smart contract vulnerabilities. And vulnerabilities in smart contracts pose great challenges for maintaining security of blockchain systems.

2   Classifications of Blockchain

In terms of its intrinsic properties, the blockchain is a system that is participated and maintained by multiple parties. Generally speaking, the blockchain can be divided into public blockchain and permissioned blockchain according to the access scope of participants. The public blockchain has no entry threshold and anyone can join the network. The consortium blockchain is a blockchain network that has an access mechanism and requires permission to join.

---

[1]Turing Completeness: In computability theory, a system of data-manipulation rules (such as a computer's instruction set, a programming language, or a cellular automation) is said to be Turing complete or computationally universal if it can be used to simulate any Turing machine. (Gannon, Paul, Colossus: Bletchley Park's Greatest Secret, London: Atlantic Books, 2006-01-10 [2006], ISBN 978–184–354-330-5)

Public Blockchain

Public blockchain is also called permissionless blockchain, which is a blockchain network with no access threshold and no access restrictions, where anyone can participate. Every user in the network can publish, verify and receive transactions on the public blockchain, and can compete for accounting rights. Moreover, the transactions pass through the consensus of nodes in the whole network, and finally all nodes can have all ledger data. The technological upgrading and maintenance of the public blockchain are all completed by the public community. General public blockchain codes are open source and subject to public review and supervision. Representative items of the public blockchain include Bitcoin and Ethereum. Bitcoin is a decentralized and difficult-to-tamper ledger that anyone can record and verify, creating a peer-to-peer electronic cash system that does not rely on central institutions. Ethereum extends the concept of bitcoin, making it a reality to run codes, verify, store and copy business data on multiple computers around the world.

From the perspective of human beings, the accounting process in public blockchain is public. All users can compete for accounting rights and check the legality of transactions; From the perspective of data, the data on the chain are open and transparent, and anyone can have a ledger of all historical data; From the perspective of codes, the governance of public blockchain (including maintenance and technology upgrading) is completed by the public community; From the perspective of the value, people who participate in the contribution can get corresponding economic rewards.

Public blockchain can provide the most general trust services for all users by making ledgers, accounting, governance and incentives public. The spontaneous trust brought by the public blockchain simply stems from the sharing principle in its design process, which provides economic incentives for gathering community and sustainable development. Those who participate in the contribution in the system can receive corresponding economic rewards. However, the public blockchain itself does not have any asset injection to pay the rewards, but the system issues a kind of "asset", that is, system tokens to pay the accounting node. Such system tokens are credentials for using system services. Therefore, the value of the assets of the public blockchain system is closely related to the robustness, application ecology, user structure, external market and investor psychology of its own system, which often fluctuates greatly, bringing room for speculation.

At present, the usage scenarios of public blockchain are relatively limited and can only be used in the fields of pure accounting and closed contracts. So it has relatively low flexibility and requires a long development process.

Permissioned Blockchain

Permissioned blockchain is a blockchain with the member control mechanism, which is mainly divided into consortium blockchain and private blockchain. At present, the consortium blockchain is the main development and application direction. The development of consortium blockchain can be traced back to 2014. Large institutions represented by R3 and Hyperledger realized that blockchain can be decoupled from bitcoin and used in various scenarios of cooperation among organizations. The paradigm of consortium blockchain gradually emerged. Consortium blockchain is a blockchain network between multi-institutional organizations with an access mechanism. Consortium blockchain is multi-central in technology, and the participating members need to pass through the access mechanism. Because the consortium blockchain generally has a small consensus range, it has better system performance.

The design of consortium blockchain makes the release, verification and reception of transaction data run among multi-institutional organizations. In general, it is only open to members of the consortium, and the relevant accounting rights depend on the consortium rules, but the final ledger data is jointly maintained by the organizations of the entire network. At the same time, the governance of the consortium blockchain is entirely decided by the consortium, which generally includes multi-party leadership or fair governance through democratic consultation. Through the realization of common ledgers, co-construction of accounting and cooperative governance among multiple organizations in the consortium, a credible foundation is established within the consortium. At the same time, multi-party redundant storage of ledger data can bring the characteristic of being difficult to tamper with, thus improving the efficiency of multi-party business collaborative operation and establishing the cornerstone of trust among institutions.

The consortium ensures efficient multi-party verification of business data through multi-party consensus on transaction data. In addition, because each organization has set up network nodes, the data can be stored in each organization in a decentralized way, and data tampering is more difficult through multi-party redundant storage. Therefore, as long as the consortium blockchain system operates stably, illegal transactions cannot pass the consensus confirmation process of all institutions, which can improve the credible flow of data among institutions.

Chapter 3
The Industrial Development Trend of Blockchain

1 Global Industrial Development Trend of Blockchain

Countries all over the World Are Competing to Lay out Blockchain and Occupy the High Ground in the Industry. And the Regulatory System Has Been Improving

Blockchain technology will have a profound impact on social and economic development in the next 10–15 years. According to the report *Blockchain Now and Tomorrow* by the European Commission's Joint Research Centre,[1] the global investment in blockchain start-ups was 45 million euros in 2014, 3.9 billion euros in 2017 and 7.4 billion euros in 2018, which showed a steady increasing trend. The growth in investment has also brought about a sharp increase in the number of start-ups in the global blockchain field.

In the growth trend of the number of blockchain start-ups shown in Fig. 3.1, by December 31, 2018, the top five countries in terms of the number of blockchain start-ups were respectively, the United States ranked first with 435 companies, accounting for 28% of the global blockchain start-up ecosystem; second was China with 333 companies, accounting for 28%; the European Union ranked the third with 187 companies, accounting for 15%; fourth was Canada with 28 companies, accounting for 2%; and Israel ranked the fifth with 21 companies, accounting for 2%.

More than half of the world's well-known blockchain start-ups came from the United States, covering the whole industrial chain of the blockchain, such as the digital asset exchange, Coinbase, the digital currency storage and exchange app, Circle, cross-border payment app, Ripple, the cross-chain trading platform,

---

[1] Nascimento, Susana, et al. "Blockchain Now And Tomorrow-Assessing Multidimensional impacts of Distributed Ledger Technologies." European Union, Joint Research Centre. Luxembourg: Publications Office of the European Union.

Center for Electronics and Information Studies, Chinese Academy of Engineering, *The Development of Blockchain Technology*, https://doi.org/10.1007/978-981-16-7236-1_3

Fig. 3.1 Numbers and shares of blockchain start-ups established in the following areas from 2009 to 2018. Source: Blockchain Now and Tomorrow, European Commission's Joint Research Centre, 2019

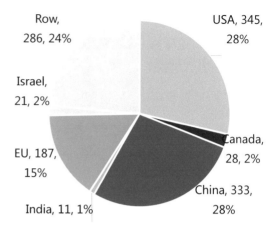

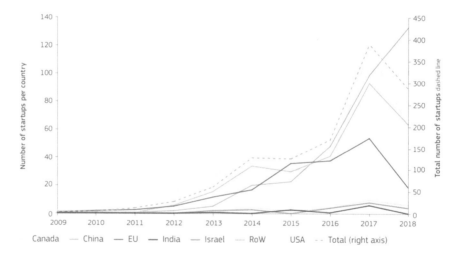

Fig. 3.2 Trends in the total number of global major players in blockchain start-ups. Source: Blockchain Now and Tomorrow, European Commission's Joint Research Centre, 2019

Blockstream, the financial blockchain app, Filecoin, Chain, Skuchain, Stellar, PeerNova, Align Commerce, Bitfury, Augur, Veem, Blockai, Chronicled, BlockCypher, OX, ShoCard, Uphold, etc.

The report shows that from 2010 to 2017, the number of start-ups in the global blockchain industry grew most rapidly in the United States, China and Europe. Globally, it maintained an annual growth rate of about 40%. However, in 2018, the global growth rate began to show a sharp decline. China was the only country to see an increase in the number of blockchain start-ups[2] (as shown in Fig. 3.2).

---

[2]*Blockchain Now and Tomorrow*, European Commission, *Information Security and Communication Confidentiality Information Security and Communications Privacy*, 2019-12-10

The report, *Blockchain Now and Tomorrow* by the European Commission's Joint Research Centre, also shows that the economic activities currently mainly engaged in by global blockchain start-ups can be divided into two categories. One is the companies involved in "Business and Financial Service", with a number of 672. Their economic activities include financial payment, data management, transaction processing, investment, advertising and marketing. The other is companies involved in "Information Technology", with a number of 568. These companies are IT companies that develop software for vertical market applications, enterprise applications, databases, network management and healthcare. The distributions of blockchain start-ups are as shown in Fig. 3.3.

By analyzing the segmentation of start-ups in the global blockchain industry, we can find that China is one of the leaders in the number of start-ups, and the business distribution involved in start-ups is also diversified. As can be seen in Fig. 3.4, about 35% of enterprises are engaged in financial institutions and services, about 16% in consumer information services, about 16% in related business support, and about

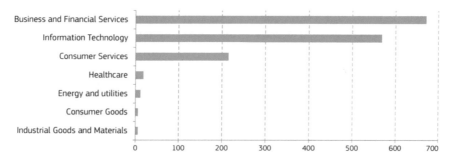

Fig. 3.3 Distribution of blockchain start-ups. Source: Blockchain Now and Tomorrow, European Commission's Joint Research Centre, 2019

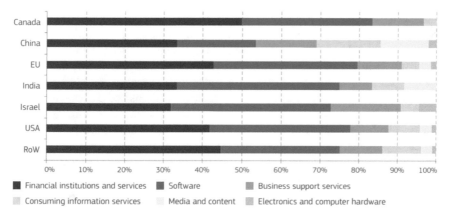

Fig. 3.4 Industrial profile of start-ups in global major players (2009–2018). Source: Blockchain Now and Tomorrow, European Commission's Joint Research Centre, 2019

12% in media and content production. Generally speaking, blockchain companies in china focus on blockchain applications, most of which are related to consumer applications. The distribution of other blockchain industries in countries except China does not show a trend of diversification, but convergence. For example, in the United States and the European Union, more than 70% of start-ups are focused on the development of financial service software and related software, and 10% are engaged in other industries such as consumer information services and media.

Before 2019, the supervision of governments was significantly slower than that of the market. The Facebook Libra in 2019 triggered a change in the attitude of global governments towards blockchain and cryptocurrency regulation. On June 2019, Facebook released the White Paper on Libra. Libra is a cryptocurrency initiative from Facebook, which sparked disputes among global regulators and stimulated regulatory consciousness around the world. At present, financial regulators in many countries have clearly vocalized their opposition to Libra. At the same time, governments have also begun to change their attitudes and are becoming active in regulating the development of the blockchain industry.

The U.S. Government maintains a cautious regulatory attitude towards blockchain technology. On the one hand, the U.S. Government affirms the application potential of blockchain technology innovation, and on the other hand, it is also exploring regulatory policies for cryptocurrencies. From 2018 to 2019, both houses of congress held at least six hearings to discuss the definition of the cryptocurrency and the challenges it poses to asset supervision. In 2019, U.S. Securities and Exchange Commission (SEC), Commodity Futures Trading Commission (CFTC) and the Congress successively issued some guidelines, providing a road map for the development of the US blockchain and digital currency regulations in 2020.

In April 2019, the U.S. Securities and Exchange Commission issued the guidelines for Token to explain some of the elements of how regulators identify digital assets as securities. In July, *Blockchain Promotion Act of 2019* was approved by the Congress, which is very important to maintain its leadship in blockchain technology innovation and application.[3] According to the bill, the federal government would promote the in-depth application of blockchain technology in non-financial fields. At the same time, the government would also set up a blockchain working group to promote the development and unification of blockchain technology definitions and standards. In July, CFTC approved bitcoin futures contracts provided by derivatives trading platform, LedgerX, for physical settlement, approved the application of encrypted derivatives supplier, ErisX, and granted the license of Derivatives Clearing Organization (DCO), which meant ErisX can now launch cryptocurrency futures products with the support of U.S. Regulators. In December, Forbes published an article saying that the U.S. Congress was drafting and discussing the *Crypto-Currency Act of 2020*, which aimed to clarify which federal agencies can regulate digital assets.

---

[3]Liu Xizi: *Inspiration from Blockchain Promotion Act of 2019 Approved by the U.S.*, *China Information World*, 2019-12-02

Fig. 3.5 Survey of attitudes of US States towards blockchain technology. Source: Brookings, 2019 (Desouza, Kevin, Chen Ye, and K. Somvanshi. "Blockchain and US state governments: An initial assessment." Techtank, Brookings Institute (2018))

States in the US set regulatory policies based on the development of their own digital economy, resulting in diversified attitudes towards blockchain in the country (as shown in Fig. 3.5). On the whole, the regulatory direction can be summarized into three aspects. One is to recognize the effectiveness of blockchain technology and its application in commercial and digital signatures. For example, Washington State amended its legislation to provide a definition for blockchain technology. The Nevada's bill requires all state agencies to accept blockchain records as a substitute for routine records and to accept companies registered in Nevada to use the blockchain to keep all business records and company documents. The second is to define the cryptocurrency. In the bills in Nevada and Colorado, virtual currency is an intangible product and is not subject to current tax laws. Wyoming classifies digital assets as property, while Montana defines utility token as digital units created and recorded in the blockchain that can be traded without the participation of third parties. The third is to encourage the application and development of blockchain technology. Nevada provides temporary regulatory exemptions that allow startups to determine the market feasibility of their products. Illinois allows local government entities to use blockchain-related services within the scope permitted by law.

The rapid development of blockchain technology has also received attention from the European Union in terms of policy regulation. Initially, EU policies focused on crypto assets. In November 2016, the European Commission and the European Parliament set up a special group on fintech distributed ledger technology. In March 2017, the European Commission convened a public consultation meeting on fintech, with the aim of soliciting opinions on fintech development policies from stakeholders. In March 2018, the European Commission issued FinTech Action Plan, which held that blockchain technology was at an early stage of development and too broad legislative or regulatory actions were not appropriate. Therefore, the plan only defined basic technical conditions, so as not to stifle innovation. Based on the action plan, the EU has successively issued a large number of targeted mechanisms, such as establishing best practices in the EU blockchain and setting up general principles and standards with Regulatory Sandbox.

During OECD Global Blockchain Policy Forum in September 2019, the European Commission's Joint Research Centre published *Blockchain Now and Tomorrow*. The report was prepared by 14 researchers from the European Commission's Joint Research Centre. Some researchers believed that the report showed that the EU has realized the extensive changes and profound impacts of the blockchain on the economies, industries and societies at present and in the future, while the EU's attention to blockchain technology had never been raised to the policy level before. This report explored a multi-dimensional analysis of the application and potential application of blockchain technology in many fields. The report showed that European policy makers are looking for solutions for the blockchain. The European Commission is helping multi-stakeholder to collect initiatives from industries, startups, governments, international organizations and societies, which covered a range of applications, including access management data, real-time report, identity management and supply chains.

The participation of EU countries in blockchain supervision is also increasing. Britain is unique in terms of supervision. In 2015, Britain introduced the Regulatory Sandbox to control new risks in the Fintech field, including the blockchain, and to continuously encourage technological innovation. In January 2016, the British government released an important report on blockchain technology - *Distributed Ledger Technology: Beyond Block Chain*, which was the only blockchain report released by a government in the world at that time. In 2019, Britain formulated the final guidelines for the supervision of crypto assets, specifying which tokens fell under its jurisdiction. This was the first formal guidelines for the supervision of crypto assets in the world. France also issued a new encryption law "PACTE" in 2019, granting the blockchain start-ups of the right to open bank accounts under supervision. The German Federal Government officially released the *Blockchain-Strategie der Bundesregierung* in September 2019, which defined the measures of blockchain technology in Germany. These measures include facilitating the stability and innovation of the blockchain in the financial industry through legislation, promoting the application of projects in the energy industry, administrative projects, digital identities, sustainable projects and other fields, exploring the construction of a new legal framework under the blockchain cooperation mode, actively pushing forward the technical standards and certification of the blockchain, and expediting the exchange of talents and technologies in the blockchain industry.

Japan and South Korea are prominent representatives of the development of the blockchain in Asian countries. Japan has formed a multi-lateral cooperation mechanism among the government, financial institutions, listed enterprises and traditional enterprises in the field of blockchain at the legal level, infrastructure level and application level. The Japanese government has continuously improved the licensing mechanism for trading platforms, stipulating that commercial blockchain scenarios must be subject to mandatory registration by national regulatory authorities to promote compliance for blockchain projects. Generally speaking, Japan supports the development of various applications of blockchain and takes the lead in blockchain supervision in the world. South Korea currently supervises digital asset trading platforms in the same way as it regulates traditional banks, and the supervision of digital asset circulation has been gradually relaxed since 2018. At the same time, due to South Korea's unique economic system (that is, large enterprises control the economic lifeline), most compliant blockchain projects are supported by large enterprises.

Australia released *The National Blockchain Roadmap* in 2019, which would strengthen the supervision and guidance, skills training and capacity building of the blockchain industry, increase industrial investment, promote international cooperation and enhance industrial competitiveness. The roadmap has integrated the blockchain into the government and financial sectors, accelerated the digital transformation of the government to ensure Australia remains a leader in this field.

NITI Aayog, a policy think tank of the Indian government, issued a national blockchain policy document draft in 2020, called "Blockchain - The India Strategy". The strategy document focused on stakeholders such as the government, business leaders and citizens, and aimed to clarify the concepts of blockchain technology and formulate a specific national action plan for blockchain technology. The policy document was divided into two parts. The first part involved basic concepts, trust systems, smart contracts and the economic potential of blockchain, usability of businesses and different ongoing cases. NITI Aayog said that proof of concepts had been carried out in four areas to better understand the obstacles that may be encountered in implementing blockchain technology. Pilot projects include tracking of drug supply chains, verification and approval of claims for fertilizer subsidy expenditures, verification of university certificates and transfer of land records. However, according to NITI Aayog, in order to deploy the blockchain on a large scale, the private and public sectors would need some legal and regulatory changes. The second part of the strategy focused on the proposal to build a dynamic blockchain ecosystem in India, including regulatory and policy considerations, policy solutions to establish national infrastructure, and the adoption of blockchain technology in the procurement process of government agencies.

The Integration of Blockchain and Real Economy Proves to Be a Main Trend. And Giant Companies Have Joined in

The report *Blockchain Now and Tomorrow—Assessing Multidimensional Impacts of Distributed Ledger Technologies* by European Commission's Joint Research Centre pointed out that blockchain technology has had and will have a wide-ranging impact on global industry, economy and society. Although blockchain was once hyped and exaggerated, now, the influence of this technology on various industries has gradually begun to emerge and will become one of the technologies that will have a profound impact on the global industry and society in the next 10–15 years.

The report analyzed the practical application of blockchain technology in finance, trade, supply chain, intelligent manufacturing, energy, digital content, medical and health care, government and public services and other fields worldwide. The report concluded that blockchain technology has three main advantages. One is to reduce intermediate transaction costs and improve transaction efficiency and security. Santander Bank of Spain has predicted that blockchain technology will help the global banking industry save 15 billion to 20 billion dollars in infrastructure investment every year. The second is to improve data transparency and security, realize the traceability of data and prevent data diddling. For example, blockchain-based supply chain systems can facilitate the assistance of global supply chains, including various subjects of mutual trust or distrust, such as producers, retailers, distributors, transporters and consumers. Third, smart contracts can guarantee the automatic execution of the transaction process. In the energy industry, the energy trading system based on blockchain technology and smart contracts is changing the traditional centralized energy system, making decentralized local production—local consumption possible.[4]

At present, global tech and financial giants and traditional industry magnates are speeding up the layout of blockchain. Since 2013, focusing on cryptocurrency payment and fintech, Google has invested in seven companies, such as Ripple Labs, Buttercoin. Microsoft launched the Blockchain as a Service (BaaS) in 2015 based on Azure cloud services. IBM began to invest in blockchain enterprises in 2016. In 2019, IBM began to attach importance to personal data management, digital advertising, digital asset management and other fields, and successively invested in MetaMe, Lucidity and Security. In February 2019, Facebook announced its acquisition of Chainspace, which was Facebook's first acquisition of a blockchain company. Chainspace is founded by researchers from University College London and its innovative smart contract system has been applied to the payments to improve the transaction processing speed. In June 2019, Facebook announced the launch of the cryptocurrency, Libra, which aimed to establish a simple, borderless monetary and financial infrastructure to provide borderless, low-cost and inclusive financial services to billions of people. In the financial field, financial giants of various countries began to lay out blockchain industries very early. In 2015, Goldman Sachs and JPMorgan began to invest in blockchain companies. Goldman Sachs has invested in AXONI, BitGo, Digital Asset Holdings and Circle, while JPMorgan has invested in AXONI, R3 and Digital Asset Holdings.

After years of development, the world has formed several blockchain ecological alliances led by major enterprises, involving important fields such as logistics and transportation, finance, open source software, etc. Among them, alliances focusing on the research and promotion of blockchain technology include R3, HyperLedger

---

[4]Lu Yapeng: *The Development of Global Blockchain Industry Becomes Rational, People's Posts and Telecommunications News*, 2019-12-30

and Enterprise Ethereum Alliance. R3 was established in 2014, and its blockchain ecosystem is one of the largest blockchain alliances in the world. The number of members reached 386, covering finance, education, energy, food, insurance, law and other fields. In vertical industry applications, alliances focusing on industry technology solutions have been formed, such as TradeLens, Interbank Information Network (IIN). IIN was initiated by J.P. Morgan in 2017 and currently has 345 members. It uses blockchain technology for cross-border payment and interbank information sharing. Initiated by IBM and Maersk, TradeLens has attracted more than 100 global ocean shipping enterprises and port enterprises, and its members account for 20% of the global ocean shipping market.

The Establishment of Blockchain Standard System Is Accelerating, and the Fight for Voices Is Increasingly Fierce

Since 2016, with the rapid development of blockchain technology and application, the International Standardization Organization has been studying and launching the work related to blockchain standardization. Standards organizations have accelerated the research and formulation of blockchain standards and have made much progress in some key standards, including the Telecommunication Standardization Sector of International Telecommunication Union (ITU-T) and International Standardization Organization (ISO).

In April 2016, with the help of the International Standardization Organization (ISO), the Australian Standards Association called for the establishment of a new blockchain technical committee to carry out blockchain standardization for interoperability, terminology, privacy, security and auditing. The above proposal was adopted in September 2016, and ISO appointed the Australian Standards Association as the ISO/TC 307 Secretariat. As of January 2020, 43 participating countries and 13 observing countries have set up 6 working groups, 1 task force and 1 research group, covering basics, security and privacy protection, smart contracts, governance, auditing and so on, mainly led by experts from Britain, France, the United States, Australia and other countries. At present, ISO/TC 307 has established 11 standards in terms of terminology, reference architecture, taxonomy and ontology, and a technical report *Overview of and Interactions between Smart Contracts in Blockchain and Distributed Ledger Technology Systems*.

ITU-T started the research on blockchain standardization in 2017. It has set up the Focus Group on Application of Distributed Ledger Technology, and begun to carry out research on terminologies, use cases, architectures, evaluations, securities, supervision and other aspects. In August 2019, eight research reports were completed and released. In addition, ITU-T has also set up special research groups in the 16th and 17th research groups. The 13th and 20th research groups have also initiated international standardization works related to the blockchain. At present, more than 20 international proposals have been launched, and many projects are about to enter the approval stage. The Standards Association of the Institute of Electrical and Electronics Engineers (IEEE-SA) has initiated the exploration of standards and projects in the field of blockchain since 2017. It has approved a number of standards such as *Application Framework of Blockchain in Internet of Things* and has carried out standardization research on blockchain technology in the fields of digital inclusion, digital identity, asset transaction and interoperability.

At the same time, the IEEE-SA has initiated the exploration of standards and projects in the field of blockchain since 2017. Currently, six standards have been approved. Among them, the *Standard for Data Format for Blockchain Systems* is led by Chinese experts. The World Wide Web Consortium (W3C) has launched three community groups related to the blockchain to carry out blockchain standardization activities, namely, the Blockchain community group, the blockchain digital assets community group and the interledger payments community group.

2   Analysis on the Current Situation of China's Blockchain Industry

National Strategic Orientation and Industrial Policies Have Been Continuously Improved

2016 is the first year of the development of China's blockchain. Blockchain technology has been written into the *13th Five-Year National Informatization Plan.* Government departments at all levels of the country issued various policy guidelines for the development of blockchain to promote the in-depth application of blockchain technology in all industries. From 2017 to 2018, six documents in the guidelines issued by the State Council mentioned the explicit development and utilization of blockchain technology (as shown in Table 3.1). On the other hand, strict ICO supervision policies have also been issued. On September 2017, People's Bank of China and other six ministries and commissions jointly issued the Announcement on Preventing the Financing Risks of Initial Coin Offerings, which characterized ICO as an unauthorized illegal public financing and ordered it to stop. On August 24, 2018, the five ministries and commissions jointly issued the *Risk Warning for Preventing Illegal Fundraising in the Name of "Virtual Currency" or "Blockchain"*. The document pointed out that lawbreakers, under the guise of "financial innovation "and "blockchain", used "virtual currency", "virtual assets" and "digital assets "to absorb funds, thus infringing on the legitimate rights and interests of the public. This indicates that China officially ban ICO.

2019 was a bumper year for blockchain policies in China. On October 2019, General secretary Xi Jinping stressed that the blockchain be an important breakthrough for the core technology innovation during a collective study for Political Bureau of the CPC Central Committee. We should make clear the main direction, increase investment and strive to secure a number of key core technologies and

Table 3.1 Guidance documents on "blockchain" issued by the State Council from 2016 to 2018

Time	Document	Contents
December, 2016	*Circular of the State Council on Issuing the 13th Five-Year National Informatization Plan*	Strengthening the advanced layout of strategic cutting-edge technologies, including blockchain
January, 2017	*Opinions of the General Office of the State Council on Innovating Management, Optimizing Services, Cultivating New Drivers of Economic Development and Accelerating the Conversion of New and Old Drivers*	Innovating the systems and mechanisms, breaking through the management restrictions of institutes and disciplines and building several industrial innovation centers and innovation networks in the cross-integrated fields of artificial intelligence, blockchain, energy Internet, smart manufacturing, big data applications, genetic engineering, and digital creativity
July 2017	*Notice of the State Council on Issuing the Development Plan on the New Generation of Artificial Intelligence*	Promoting the integration of blockchain technology and artificial intelligence, and establishing a new social credit system to minimize the cost and risk of interpersonal communication
August, 2017	*Guiding Opinions of the State Council on Further Expanding and Upgrading Information Consumption to Constantly Release Domestic Demand Potentials*	Encouraging the use of open-source code to develop personalized software, and carrying out pilot applications based on new technologies such as blockchain and artificial intelligence
October, 2017	*Guiding Opinions of the General Office of the State Council on Vigorously Advancing the Innovation on and Application of Supply Chains*	Studying and using blockchain, artificial intelligence and other emerging technologies to establish credit evaluation mechanisms based on supply chains
November, 2017	*Guiding Opinions of the General Office of the State Council on Deepening the "Internet + Advanced Manufacturing Industry" to Develop the Industrial Internet*	Promoting the application research and exploration of edge computing, artificial intelligence, augmented reality, virtual reality, blockchain and other emerging frontier technologies in the industrial Internet
May 2018	*Notice of the State Council on Issuing the Plan for Further Deepening the Reform and Opening up of China (Guangdong) Pilot Free Trade Zone*	Vigorously developing financial technology and accelerate the research and application of blockchain and big data technology under the premise of compliance with laws and regulations.

accelerate the development of the technology and industry innovation of the blockchain. Blockchain has become the third emerging technology learned collectively by the Political Bureau of the CPC Central Committee ranking behind big data and artificial intelligence, which reflects the central government's emphasis on blockchain technology.

On October 2019, the Standing Committee of the National People's Congress passed the *Cryptography Law of the People's Republic of China*, which have been implemented on January 1, 2020. The Law aims to standardize the application and management of cryptography, promote the development of cryptography, ensure the safety of network and information, and improve the scientific, standardized and legal level of cryptography management. It is a comprehensive and basic cryptography law in China and provides a basic legal regulatory framework for the development of cryptography. Blockchain is a distributed ledger technology based on cryptography. The launch of Cryptography Law provides important legal protection and normative guidance for China to promote the development of blockchain technology and industry.

These two major events have injected a strong impetus into the development of the blockchain industry, and facilitated the local blockchain policy evolution to enter a period of rapid development in the second half of 2019. According to statistics, the blockchain policies issued in November 2019, grew 140% month on month, and the industry's enthusiasm for development was unprecedented. At present, 17 provinces, autonomous regions and municipalities such as Beijing, Shanghai, Guangdong, Chongqing, Zhejiang, Jiangsu and Guizhou have all introduced policies related to the blockchain, which are mainly support-oriented[5]. Among them, the policies worthy of attention include: in November 2019, Guangdong Province issued the *Detailed Rules for Implementation of Several Measures of Huangpu District and Guangzhou Development District to Accelerate the Leading Reform of Blockchain Industry* and set up a 1 billion yuan blockchain industry fund; Hebei Province, Yunnan Province, Shandong Province, Jilin Province and Changchun City all proposed to speed up the layout of the blockchain and promote the development of the blockchain at the meeting of the local standing committees on November 1st.

In 2018, policies issued by various regions mostly covered finance, services, supply chains and other fields. In 2019, various ministries and local governments of China further extended the blockchain technology to other fields, such as water conservation, engineering construction, flood control, smart correction, etc., while promoting the mode transformation in existing fields, such as trading platforms, commercial systems, financial supervision, etc.

In 2020, with the deepening application of fintech and blockchain, how to handle the supervision scale has become an important issue between technological innovation and supervision. In January 2020, the first list for the pilot application of Beijing's fintech innovation supervision and the implementation plan for the construction of Shanghai fintech center were released successively. Industry insiders pointed out that it marked the formal launch of the Chinese financial "regulatory sandbox". The list of relevant policies for application and promotion of blockchain in National Ministries and Commissions is shown in Table 3.2.

The Supervisory Sandbox pilot program is to provide certain policy exemptions for blockchain-related fintech innovation projects in a strong regulatory environment, to provide a good environment for future scientific and technological

---

[5]Xin Wang: *Blockchain: Farewell to Fickleness and Deepening the Application, People's Posts and Telecommunications News*, 2020-01-20

Table 3.2 List of relevant policies for application and promotion of blockchain in National Ministries and Commissions from 2019 to 2020

Releasing subject	Releasing time	Policy/document name
CPC Central Committee and State Council	February, 2020	Document No.1 *Opinions of the CPC Central Committee and the State Council on Paying Special Attention to Key Work in the Fields of Agriculture, Rural Areas and Rural People to Ensure the Achievement of Overall Well-off as Scheduled*
Ministry of Transport, National Development and Reform Commission, Ministry of Industry and Information Technology, Ministry of Finance, Ministry of Commerce, General Administration of Customs and State Taxation Administration	February, 2020	*Guiding Opinions on Vigorously Promoting High-quality Development of Shipping Industry*
Ministry of Agriculture and Rural Affairs, Office of the Central Cyberspace Affair Commission	January, 2020	*Development Plan of Digital Agriculture and Rural Areas (2019-2025)*
General Office of the State Council	January, 2020	*Guiding Opinions on Supporting Deepening Reform and Innovation in National New Districts and Accelerating High-quality Development*
Ministry of Commerce and other seven departments	January, 2020	*Guiding Opinions on Promoting Service Outsourcing and Accelerating Transformation and Upgrading*
China Banking and Insurance Regulatory Commission	January, 2020	*Guiding Opinions on Promoting High-quality Development of Banking and Insurance Industry*
Supreme People's Court	December, 2019	*Opinions on the People's Court Providing Judicial Services and Guarantees for the Construction of China (Shanghai) Pilot Free Trade Zone Lin-gang Special Area*
Supreme People's Court	December, 2019	*Opinions on the People's Court Further Providing Judicial Services and Guarantees for the Construction of "the Belt and Road Initiative"*
CPC Central Committee and State Council	December, 2019	*Outline of Regional Integration Development Plan for Yangtze River Delta*
CPC Central Committee and State Council	November, 2019	*Guiding Opinions on Promoting High-quality Development of Trade*
State Council	September 2019	*Issue Guidance on Strengthening and Standardizing Operational and Post-operational Oversight*
CPC Central Committee and State Council	September 2019	*Program of Building a Powerful Country Through Transportation*

(continued)

Table 3.2 (continued)

Releasing subject	Releasing time	Policy/document name
Ministry of Industry and Information Technology	September 2019	*Guiding Opinions on Industrial Big Data Development (Draft for Comments)*
Ministry of Industry and Information Technology, Ministry of Education, Ministry of Human Resources and Social Security and other seven departments	August, 2019	*Notice on Printing and Distributing Guidance on Strengthening Industrial Internet Security*
State Council	August, 2019	*Notice on Printing and Distributing the Overall Plan for Six New Pilot Free Trade Zones*
Supreme People's Court	June, 2019	*Opinions on Deepening Implementation Reform and Perfecting Long-term Mechanism to Solve Implementation Difficulties-Outline of Implementation Work of People's Courts (2019-2023)*
Ministry of Industry and Information Technology	June, 2019	*2019 Work Plan of Industrial Internet Special Working Group*
Ministry of Industry and Information Technology	April, 2019	*Guidance on Strengthening Industrial Internet Security (Draft for Comments)*
National Development and Reform Commission, Ministry of Water Resources	April, 2019	*National Water Conservation Plan*
Ministry of Commerce and other 11 departments	March, 2019	*Guiding Opinions on Promoting the Development of Platform Economy in Commodity Trading Markets*
Ministry of Industry and Information Technology	March, 2019	*Implementation Plan for Selection of New Information Consumption Demonstration Projects*
National Development and Reform Commission	January, 2019	*Catalog of Industrial Structure Adjustment Guidance (2019, Draft for Comments)*

innovation. At the same time, through prior institutional arrangements, the legitimate rights and interests of financial consumers are fully protected, and the dynamic balance between financial innovation, compliance supervision and financial consumer protection is better realized.[6]

---

[6]Yue Pinyu: *The First Pilot Application and Fintech Enterprises Entering the Sandbox, Beijing Business Today*

The Standard System Has Been Initially Established and the Development of Standards Has Been Steadily Promoted

Currently, China is actively promoting blockchain industry and trying to build blockchain standard systems, including Trusted Blockchain Standards. According to incomplete statistics, there is currently one national standard related to the blockchain and more than 10 industry standards at the stage of research or approval, and a number of group standards have been issued, as follows in Table 3.3.

Main Body of Industry Continues to Grow and Upstream and Downstream Chains Are Basically Formed

According to the monitoring of data research center of the China Academy of Information and Communication Technology (CAICT), as of December 2019, there were 653 blockchain enterprises in China. Since 2014, the number of blockchain enterprises in China has sprung out rapidly, reaching its peak in 2018, with 183 new enterprises established in this year. In 2019, influenced by various aspects at home and abroad, the development of blockchain industry in China gradually returned to rationality, with 11 new blockchain enterprises established, far less than the number of previous years (as shown in Fig. 3.6).

China's blockchain enterprises are mainly concentrated in the "extensive finance" field (including finance, digital assets and supply chain finance), accounting for 43%. In addition, the Internet, traceability, supply chains & logistics, intellectual property rights, government affairs, public services, etc. are the main application fields of blockchain technology (as shown in Fig. 3.7).

In the R&D of blockchain technology, 35% of China's enterprises develop solutions based on blockchain technology; 17% of enterprises are engaged in basic protocol research, including public blockchain, private blockchain, consortium blockchain and other basic protocol technologies; 11% of enterprises provide BaaS service. In addition, there are many enterprises involved in transaction technology (digital wallet), security technology, digital identity and other fields (as shown in Fig. 3.8).

China's ICT industry and traditional industry giants are actively laying out blockchains. In 2019, Cyberspace Administration of China issued two batches of blockchain information service filing lists in accordance with the *Regulations on the Administration of Blockchain Information Services*. 422 institutions and 506 blockchain service platforms are included. By analyzing the registered enterprises on the list, it can be seen that finance, supply chain and Internet are the most concentrated areas of blockchain application. Fields such as traceability, intellectual property protection, government/public services are also involved. Filing enterprises include the Internet, financial and manufacturing giants in China. For example, Huawei, Baidu, Alibaba, Tencent, Jingdong, etc. have released BaaS service

Table 3.3 The National and Industry Standards Related to the Blockchain

No.	Standard name	Standard nature	Approval authority/ issuing organization	Current status
1	*Information Technology—Blockchain and Distributed Ledger Technology—Reference Architecture*	National standards	National Standardization Administration Committee	Draft
2	*Technical Security Specification for Financial Distributed Ledgers*	Financial Industry Standards	China Standardization Technical Committee	Issued
3	*General Technical Requirements for Blockchain*	Communication industry standards	China Communications Standardization Association	Submitted for approval
4	*General Review Index and Test Method of Blockchain System*	Communication Industry standards	China Communications Standardization Association	Submitted for approval
5	*Blockchain Application Technology Requirements—Supply Chain Finance*	Communication Industry standards	China Communications Standardization Association	Approved
6	*Blockchain Application Technology Requirements—Police Data Sharing*	Communication Industry standards	China Communications Standardization Association	Approved
7	*Blockchain Application Technology Requirements—Traceability*	Communication Industry standards	China Communications Standardization Association	Approved
8	*Blockchain Safety—Evaluation Index and Review Method*	Communication Industry standards	China Communications Standardization Association	Approved
9	*Blockchain Application Technology Requirements—Judicial Deposit*	Communication Industry standards	China Communications Standardization Association	Approved
10	*Blockchain—Service Technical Requirements*	Communication Industry standards	China Communications Standardization Association	Approved
11	*Blockchain Review Requirements—Performance Test*	Communication Industry standards	China Communications Standardization Association	Approved
12	*Judicial Blockchain Technical Requirements*	Court Industry standards	Supreme People's Court	Consultation
13	*Judicial Blockchain management standard*	Court Industry standards	Supreme People's Court	Consultation
14	*Blockchain - Reference Architecture*	Group Standards	China Electronics Standardization Association	Issued
15	*Blockchain—Data Format Specification*	Group Standards	China Electronics Standardization Association	Issued

(continued)

Table 3.3 (continued)

No.	Standard name	Standard nature	Approval authority/ issuing organization	Current status
16	*Blockchain—Intelligent Contract Implementation Specification*	Group Standards	China Electronics Standardization Association	Issued
17	*Blockchain—Deposit Application Guidelines*	Group Standards	China Electronics Standardization Association	Issued
18	*Blockchain—Privacy Protection Specifications*	Group Standards	China Electronics Standardization Association	Issued

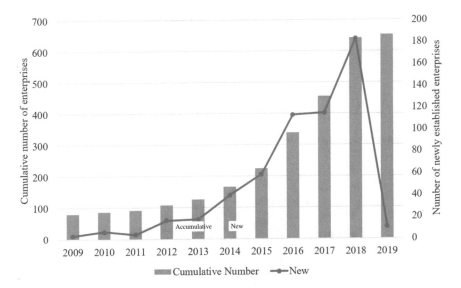

Fig. 3.6 Growth trend of China's blockchain enterprises

platforms; Industrial and Commercial Bank of China, PingAn Bank, Bank of Jiangsu, Suning Bank. etc. have released financial blockchain service platforms; Midea Group, Aisino Corporation, etc. have released electronic certificate blockchain service platforms.[7]

In addition, China's science and technology giants have actively invested abroad and laid out key areas based on their existing advantages. Tencent focuses on product traceability. In September 2019, it announced its investment in Everledger, a UK blockchain startup. Everledger takes advantage of blockchain technology to

---

[7]Lu Yapeng, *Global Blockchain Industry Returns to Rational Development, People's Posts and Telecommunications News*, 2019-12-30

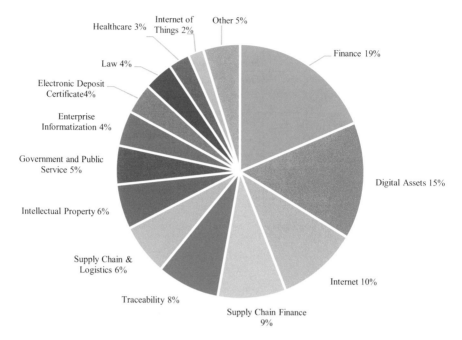

Fig. 3.7   Industrial application distribution of China's Blockchain Enterprises

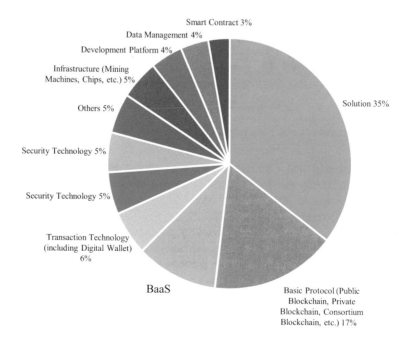

Fig. 3.8   Distribution of China's Blockchain Enterprises in technology fields

establish digital signs for specific commodities so as to realize the identification and traceability of commodities. Alibaba pays attention to product evaluation in e-commerce and privacy protection in financial services. In September 2019, it participated in Bitmark's Series A funding of US $3 million. Bitmark is a Taiwanese startup. It develops a distributed evaluation platform that can manage the evaluation of users, products and services. In May 2019, Alibaba participated in Qedit's Series A funding of USD ten million. Qedit is an Israeli startup that develops enterprise-level user data privacy protection technology.

At the same time, a number of startups with certain technological competitiveness in the blockchain industry has also been established in China such as Hangzhou Fuzamei Technology Co., Ltd., Hangzhou Qulian Technology Co., Ltd., ZhongAn Information Technology Service Co., Ltd. and other new technology start-ups. China also ranks high in terms of the number of blockchain patent applications.

Chapter 4
Blockchain Technology Innovation Hot Spots

After more than ten years of development, blockchain technology has expanded its huge application space from the application in virtual currency to various business use cases. But at the same time, the existing blockchain technology cannot support large-scale commercial applications and the mainstream blockchain platforms also exists bottlenecks and problems, which drives the industry to continuously push the technical boundaries and innovate new technical schemes of the blockchain, including blockchain scalability, blockchain interoperability, blockchain privacy protection and security, blockchain governance technology, etc. Many of the problems listed above are continuously promoting the iterative evolution of blockchain technology, which is the current hot spots of blockchain technology innovation and deserves our continuous attention.

1 Blockchain Scalability

The main technical bottlenecks of blockchain system are performance and efficiency. Low performance brings many problems, such as transaction processing delay and corresponding costs, and makes it difficult to support large-scale user volume. This limits the development of more meaningful applications of the blockchain system. The blockchain is committed to achieving security and fairness of transactions, and high consistency, tamper resistance, maliciousness prevention and traceability of data under a distributed network environment lacking mutual trust. So one of the costs is performance and efficiency. This leads to the so-called Impossible trinity model of the blockchain, that is, scalability, decentralization and security cannot be achieved at the same time. Only two of the three can be taken, and they need to be balanced. However, in order to support the upper-level services, the blockchain system should still provide a good user experience when the pageview expands, and the blockchain needs to seek breakthroughs for scalability in specific application scenarios.

The current optimization idea includes replacing the traditional blockchain data structure with tree topology data structure in the ledger. In some scenarios with few related transactions, concurrent blocks can be processed synchronously, and blocks can be organized into a non-chained directed acyclic graph (DAG) structure. Through such technology, multiple blocks can be connected to one block to increase the proportion of effective blocks, thus improving the overall throughput of the system, reducing the delay of transaction confirmation, and improving the blockchain scalability to a certain extent.

The second common idea is the parallel sharing scheme. The sharing theory supports database sharing technology. Traditional database sharing is mainly used for optimization of large commercial databases, whose concept is to divide the data in a large database into many data sharing, and then store them in different servers respectively, reducing the data access pressure of each server and improving the performance of the whole database system.

The sharing of blockchain is to try to make the blockchain parallel, divides it into multiple sharing blockchains, and then allocates transactions to different sharings for execution through a load distribution mechanism. Each sharing operates independently and has an independent consensus mechanism. It supports relatively strong horizontal expansion and on-demand expansion through parallel schemes. The realization of sharing technology will bring higher cooperation efficiency and more credible production mode to the development of various transaction activities in the blockchain. However, the difficulty of this scheme lies in the transaction confirmation across-sharing and the security guarantee between the sharings. Therefore, it is really a huge challenge to integrate the sharing theory and the security theory of blockchain, including the cryptoeconomics design and the incentive mechanism design, to realize a secure, scalable and high-performance blockchain. Sharing technology includes Network Sharing, Transaction Sharing and State Sharing:

Network Sharing: Messages requiring sharing are only propagated in the internal sharing network;

Transaction Sharing: Different transactions will only run in different sharing, and each sharing will run an independent consensus algorithm;

State Sharing: Sharing is required maintain only the state data inside it and does not need to save the data of other sharings.

Permissioned blockchain generally corresponds to multi-chain and multi-channel mode. And its network scale is generally smaller than permissionless blockchain because of the entry threshold. Corresponding sub-chains or sub-channels can be created for different services in the consortium so different services can run on different blockchains. The idea of divide and conquer is adopted to improve the scalability of the overall network.

The third common idea is the upgrade and evolution of consensus algorithms. Consensus algorithms are used to coordinate the behavior of nodes in the system and maintain data consistency. Distributed systems built in untrusted environments are prone to data state inconsistency between nodes due to the unreliability of nodes themselves and the instability of communication between nodes, and even the information forged by them for malicious response. With consensus algorithms, the blockchain coordinates the behaviors and states of multiple nodes that do not trust each other, thus forming a reliable system in an untrusted environment.

In the early stage of blockchain development, the mainstream blockchain networks are mostly based on consensus algorithms of PoW (Proof of Work). Due to the waste of resources in PoW, the research on consensus algorithms based on PoS (proof of Stake) has developed rapidly since 2017. Single consensus algorithm has its own limitations, such as low efficiency of PoW consensus and low decentralization of DPoS. Blockchain researchers try to integrate two or more consensus algorithms to complement each other and select appropriate algorithms at different execution stages to achieve better consensus efficiency as a whole. At the same time, in terms of a single consensus algorithm, such as the Byzantine fault tolerance consensus that is most used in permissioned blockchain scenarios, there is a certain optimization space by improving parallelism and reducing network message traffic, which can greatly improve system performance and support most business scenarios.

Meanwhile, due to the increasing of business requirements, the amount of data on the blockchain greatly increases. Chain accumulation methods are used to manage the growing data storage on the blockchain. However, the storage requirements are increasing as more transactions recorded on the blockchain, and there is no upper limit. And for full nodes, more storage resources are needed, which will raise the threshold for full nodes and reduce number of full nodes and the concentration degree of node distribution. As more blockchain based applications emerge, there will be more data on the blockchain, which will bring more operation and maintenance costs. Besides, data migration will be very complicated. Recently, on-chain storage methods are with good scalability and have been a new research hot topic in the industry.

In order to improve the scalability of on-chain storage, solutions are as follows:

Replacing the single-node storage with multi-node distributed storage, which isolates storage from calculation, thus relieving node pressure.

Maintaining the latest state of blockchain dynamics and abandoning maintaining the state corresponding to different blockchain heights. In order to pursue performance and storage scalability, reduce the traceability efficiency of on-chain data to facilitating on-chain data clipping. The on-chain logic mainly focuses on transactional and consistency, and the work related to query and traceability is done outside the chain.

In short, with the continuous development of blockchain technology, the scalability of on-chain storage needs to be strengthened to support the scenario of business data explosion.

2 Blockchain Interoperability

"The Internet is a network of free circulation of information, while the blockchain is a network of free circulation of value". This is a good vision for the blockchain. At present, the blockchain cannot achieve efficient communication and is not a network of free circulation. Analogy with the computer network that existed in the form of local area network in the 1960s, it could not be interconnected with computers outside the local area network. Until 1969, the American Advanced Research Projects Agency (ARPA) put into use the ARPAnet with four nodes and computers had the networking capability in a homogeneous environment for the first time. In the 1980s, the birth of TCP/IP protocol enabled heterogeneous networks to interconnect with each other and accelerated the explosive development of the Internet. Returning to the blockchain, with the development of technologies, a large number of projects have emerged, but most of them are highly heterogeneous. In the early stage of development, more emphasis is placed on their own technological innovation and ecological construction, and different blockchain networks are isolated and have no communication mechanisms. As there are more and more different kinds of blockchain systems, blockchain interoperability become more and more important and significant. Blockchain interoperability technologies can help to promote data flow, value flow and cooperative work among those blockchains.

Hash-locking, Notary Scheme, Sidechain, Relay Chain, etc. are of most popular interoperability technologies (as shown in Table 4.1). Currently, the application

Table 4.1 Performance comparison of interoperability related technologies

	Hash lockdown	Notary scheme	Sidechain	Relay chain
Trust model	Blockchain self-security	Most honest notaries	Blockchain self-security	Most honest relay chain verifiers or the access blockchain self-security
Classification of messages being delivered	Assets only	Unlimited	Unlimited	Unlimited
Number of participating blockchain	Dual-chain	Connecting intermediate routing to implement multi-chain	Dual-chain	Multi-chain
Difficulty	Easy	Middle	Middle	Challenge
Limitation	The scenario is not various, and the initiator has the initiative, and can choose the opportunity to complete the transaction arbitrage	Depending on the third-party notary group	Validity verification requires block data structure	Suitable for blockchains with absolute consensus

scenario has been transmitting from dual-chain asset interoperability to full-state free circulation among multi-chain. Relay chain is a kind of interoperability that integrates notary scheme and sidechain, and has great influence in the new blockchain interoperability platform. Besides, it is still necessary to carry out convergence design for relevant components technically, such as unifying the input and output of cross-chain messages for each blockchain, constructing standard message formats, and designing efficient and verifiable data structures. What's more, improving the user interaction experience of application layer and enhancing interoperability between on-chain and off-chain world is also necessary. However, blockchain interoperability is still at very early stage.

3 Blockchain Privacy Protection and Security

Normally, the data on the blockchain is publicly visible to all participants, but in a large number of business scenarios, the exposure of data does not comply with business rules and regulatory requirements. Therefore, it is necessary to study the on-chain privacy protection technology to realize the security and controllability of data.

In a perfect privacy system, only both parties involved in the transaction know the relevant information. Moreover, they cannot obtain any other information except the transaction. Traditional cash transactions have extremely high privacy, while each transaction under bank transfer and e-payment is visible to banks and related institutions, so it has to rely on the self-discipline of centralized institutions to ensure the privacy of users.

At present, blockchain privacy protection is mainly promoted from cryptography and engineering. In terms of the permissionless blockchain, while the committer verifies the legitimacy of the transaction, it protects sensitive information such as transaction address and data through cryptography generally, such as ring signatures, blind signatures, confidential transaction, zero-knowledge proofs and other algorithms. As for the permissioned blockchain, it takes into account both and combines cryptographic means, such as secure multi-party computation. On the other hand, in engineering, methods such as private transactions and multi-subchain ledger isolation are adopted to focus on improving efficiency and save computing resources. At the same time, regulatory and authorization tracking should be considered.

Regarding the security of the blockchain, with the deepening of theoretical research, while the blockchain shows vigorous vitality, its own security problems gradually emerge. Although the blockchain provides reliable security protection in the underlying technologies, attackers can still find vulnerabilities in the blockchain system and attack them. At present, the development of blockchain application urgently requires the security research of the system and a variety of technical measures should be adopted to ensure the security of blockchain, such as ledger data security, cryptographic algorithms security, network communication security, smart contracts security, and hardware security.

Ledger data: To maintain consistency and availability of ledger data, schemes like data verification, data disaster tolerance and backup are widely adopted to ensure the consistency of each node data in the process of storing on blockchains and timely recovery of on-chain data after being lost or damaged due to system failure.

Cryptographic algorithm: With the popularization of blockchain technology in areas with strong demand for data security, such as supply chain finance, judicial deposit and government data sharing, state secret encryption gradually becomes the mainstream for blockchain application in signature verification, on-chain data access and other business processes.

Network communication: Sharing threat of attackers taking advantage of network protocol vulnerabilities to carry out eclipse attacks, routing attacks and DDoS (Distributed Denial of Service) attacks are continuously increasing.

Smart contract: Smart contract vulnerabilities are main security threats for smart contracts and blockchain applications, including contract code vulnerabilities, business logic vulnerabilities, contract operation environment problems and interface vulnerabilities. With the improvement of formal verification technology and code audit methods, security incidents caused by contract vulnerabilities are also reduced.

Hardware: To better balance the contradiction between security and performance and prevent code from being tampered with during operation, hardware security is key to blockchain security. Trusted Execution Environment (TEE) is among current main stream protection solutions, which can provide a protected secure storage and execution environment for on-chain data and intermediate data. TEE based schemes realize feasible data security protection schemes with fast speed and low cost in the blockchain.

4 Blockchain Governance Technology

The governance of blockchain technology is important to maintain the stable operation of the blockchain network. As time goes on, the original design and rules of the blockchain may no longer meet the current needs. In order to better adapt to the environment, the blockchain system needs to be continuously modified and upgraded. However, because the blockchain has the characteristics of decentralization and multi-organization member participation whose interests are different, differences often occur in the process of modification and upgrading of blockchain protocols and code rules. In severe cases, the network cannot operate normally and cause division. Therefore, the design of a reasonable and efficient governance framework contributes to reducing network splits and chaos. Meanwhile, it can improve the efficiency of software update and iteration, making the blockchain protocol adapt to the changing environment, and improving the participation of community members.

For permissionless blockchains, governance ecology usually consists of four roles: blockchain protocol developers, miners, upper-level application developers and users. Participants all have different interest demands, so it is especially important to coordinate the interest demands of participants. A mature blockchain ecology should be that all participants involved are independent and restrict each other, and none of them has absolute rights. Although no participant has the right to make decisions alone, they keep playing games with each other through the exercise of their respective rights and finally achieve a dynamic balance.

Due to the complexity of the permissionless blockchain ecology, any single participant cannot determine the direction and development of it and important decisions are made through negotiation. From the perspective of decision-making mode, the governance of the permissionless blockchain includes on-chain and off-chain governance. On-chain governance refers to a governance mode in which the negotiation and decision-making process of network upgrade and iteration is completely embedded in the blockchain system and completed by a set of automated mechanisms. Off-chain governance is a governance mode in which the decision-making process does not occur on the blockchain system but is carried out around open source communities and foundations. However, in terms of the current permissionless blockchain governance, all parties have misunderstanding in the system design concept, blockchain rule setting and other aspects, resulting in asymmetric information and other situations, which are likely to cause speculation and speculation scams.

For the permissioned blockchain, while participating in the division of labor and cooperation, all parties need to perform their own duties in the process of blockchain cold start and blockchain execution. Efficient governance of the permissioned blockchain can enhance the fairness of multi-party business collaboration which is generally divided into user system, authority management, blockchain cold start governance, blockchain run-time governance. At present, the blockchain cold start is mostly led by super administrators. However, how to reasonably implement democratic upgrading of smart contracts, safe modification of blockchain rules, node scaling, etc. in the process of blockchain execution will become the direction of exploration and improvement of the permissioned blockchain in the next step.

Chapter 5
Hot Spots and Highlights of China's Blockchain Development

1 Blockchain Underlying Platforms Are Emerging, and the Technology Is Improving

The blockchain technology research in China has been paid more attention, with increasing scientific research institutions and growing enterprise research teams. Since 2016, China's blockchain technology has developed rapidly. Research and innovation achievements on the underlying technology of the blockchain have emerged continuously, and relevant research institutions have also continued to grow. At present, there are more than 80 blockchain research institutions in China, which are mainly universities and enterprises, and located in Beijing, Hangzhou, Shanghai, Shenzhen, Guiyang and other cities. In January 2017, the People's Bank of China formally established the Digital Currency Research Institute to deploy research work in digital currency and applied for a number of digital currency-related patents.

Important achievements have been made in the blockchain technological innovation in China. The consortium blockchain and public blockchain systems have been continuously improved and industry standards have become more mature. The domestic research teams have made innovations and breakthroughs in underlying platforms and a series of core technologies such as consensus algorithm, password security, performance security, etc. They have also made certain progress in a series of key technologies such as scalability, interoperability, privacy protection and security, blockchain governance technology, etc.

China's self-developed blockchain platforms continue to emerge (as shown in Table 5.1). With the development of blockchain industry, major enterprises have increased their development investment, and autonomous blockchain underlying platforms continue to emerge. Representative platforms include Hyperchain, an underlying platform of Hangzhou Qulian Technology Co., Ltd., Ant Blockchain Underlying Platform, self-developed by Ant Financial Services Group, and

Center for Electronics and Information Studies, Chinese Academy of Engineering, *The Development of Blockchain Technology*, https://doi.org/10.1007/978-981-16-7236-1_5

Table 5.1 China's blockchain product list (in no particular order)

Enterprise name	Main product
Beijing Qihoo Technology Co., Ltd.	QBaas
Jingdong Digits Technology Holding Co., Ltd.	JD Blockchain Open Platform
ZTE Corporation	Zchain, Zchain BaaS
Union Mobile financial technology co., ltd.	UChains, UC BaaS, Supply Chain Finance Platform, Cross-border Factoring Financing Management Platform, Financial Virtual Simulation Laboratory, Non-bank Financial Institution Supervision Platform
Tencent Technology (Shenzhen) Co., Ltd.	Blockchain Electronic Invoice Scheme, Zhi Xin Chain
Tencent Cloud Computing (Beijing) Co., Ltd.	TBaaS, WeIdentify, Shuliantong and Rongziyi
Shanghai Insurance Exchange Co., Ltd.	Insurance Exchange Chain
Huawei Technologies Co., Ltd.	Beijing Big Data Catalog Chain System, Huaneng Intelligent Chain Supply Chain Service Platform
Baidu Online Network Technology (Beijing) Co., Ltd.	XuperChain
China United Network Communications Group Co., Ltd.	BaaS Platform, Data Right Confirmation Platform
China Mobile Communications Group Co., Ltd.	CMBaaS, Blockchain PKI system
Bubi (Beijing) Technologies Co., Ltd.	Bubichain, Yinuojr.cn Financial Service Platform
Cryptape Co., Ltd.	CITA, a self-developed enterprise-level blockchain underlying open source framework
Hangzhou Qulian Technology Co., Ltd.	Filoop Platform, Filoop Stamp Platform, Hyperchain, BitXMesh, BitXHub, MeshSec
ICBC Tech Co., Ltd.	ICBC Seal Chain
Beijing Ksyun Network Technology Co., Ltd.	KBaaS, Ksyun Financial Service Platform
PEOGOO Co., Ltd.	Basechain, Distributed Digital Identity System, Pbaas, Zhihui Sugar—Children's Growth Education System, Distributed Trusted Cloud Platform, Enterprise Digital Assessment System
Xi'an Zhigui Internet Technology Co., Ltd.	Xinhuitong, Zhishu Rubik's Cube, Z-BaaS, Zhigui Copyright
Zhejiang Ant Small and Micro Financial Services Group Co., Ltd.	Ant Blockchain Platform
State Grid Electronic Commerce Co., Ltd.	E-commerce Blockchain, Central Enterprises E-commerce Consortium Blockchain, State Grid Blockchain
Neusoft Corporation	SaCa EchoTrust
SF Technology Co., Ltd.	Big Data Platform, Data Beacon, Feng Bao Display, SF Trace Blockchain
Jiangsu Rongzer Information Technology Co., Ltd.	Rongzer Blockchain Government Coordination Platform, Rongzer Blockchain Precision Financial Platform, RBC, RBAAS

Source: China Academy of Information and Communication Technology, 2019

TrustSQL Platform of Tencent Blockchain. Besides, WeBank initiated the establishment of the Financial Blockchain Shenzhen Consortium and cooperated with related enterprises to establish BCOS and FISCO BCOS; in the first half of 2019, JD Chain, the underlying engine of JD Blockchain, officially opened source and launched an open source community simultaneously; Baidu released XuperChain, a self-developed underlying blockchain technology, and officially opened source.

According to the functional test results of nearly 40 enterprise underlying platforms tested by the Trusted Blockchain Initiatives in 2018 and 2019, the self-developed blockchain underlying platforms accounted for 50% of all test manufacturers in 2019, and the degree of autonomy was improved compared with 35% of the data in 2018.

The blockchain patents in China are increasing, the fields of patent are expanding, and the patent applicants are increasing. From 2013 to December 20, 2018, the total number of published blockchain patent applications worldwide were 8996 (7347 merged congeners) and China's blockchain patent applications were 4435 (4156 merged congeners). Due to the lag of patent disclosure, there were more existing blockchain patents. From 2013 to 2018, the average annual growth rate of global blockchain patents was 276%, and that of China was 321%.

China enjoys the largest number of blockchain patents in Asia, 85% of which are applied by mainland China, highlighting the market position of China's blockchain in the future. The rapid growth of blockchain patents in China not only represents the vitality of China's blockchain and the emphasis on high-tech technologies, but also indicates that China will have more voice in the field of blockchain and its international standing will be further improved.

2 Integrate Deeply with the Real Economy, and Develop More Applications

Regions have actively issued relevant policies, with clearer emphasis and specific plans. According to statistics from CAICT, during the NPC and CPPCC sessions in 2019, representatives from all over the country submitted more than 30 proposals and views about the blockchain. As of May 2019, more than 30 provinces, cities and regions, including Beijing, Shanghai, Guangdong, Jiangsu, Zhejiang, Guizhou, and Shandong, have issued policy guidance documents to develop the layout of the blockchain industry chain (as shown in Table 5.2).[1]

In 2018, cities issued special policies which aimed at cultivating the blockchain industrial ecology. According to the feedback of projects launched in 2018, local governments were more rigorous and pragmatic towards the blockchain in 2019. They focused on how to combine the blockchain technology with local

---

[1] *Blockchain White Paper (2019)*, China Academy of Information and Communication Technology, 2019-11-08

Table 5.2 Local blockchain projects in China

Province/city	Time	Content
Beijing	2018.6	The National Industrial and Information Security Center released an electronic data security platform, which used the blockchain for verification and traceability
	2018.12	Shunyi District Housing and Urban-Rural Development Committee launched the "Intelligent Supervision Information Platform for the Full Life Cycle of Shantytowns Transformation Project"
	2018.12	Beijing Internet Court officially launched the "Tianping Blockchain"
	2019.1	Baidu upgraded Beijing Haidian Park through technologies such as the blockchain and launched the first AI park in China
	2019.4	Haidian District of Beijing realized the simultaneous processing of "real estate registration + electricity transfer" businesses in second-hand housing transactions and Beijing-registered stocking housing transactions and other scenarios through technologies such as the blockchain
Hangzhou	2018.3	Hangzhou Blockchain Technology Research Institute of Zhongchao Credit Card Industry Development Co., Ltd. released BROP. It committed to the establishment of digital identities, trusted data and digital certificates based on blockchain technology to realize trusted cooperation
	2018.9	The judicial blockchain system operated by Hangzhou Internet Court was officially launched
	2018.9	Jianggan District Court of Hangzhou Municipality held the first creditors' meeting of Hangzhou Big World Hardware City Co., Ltd. The online voting data of the meeting were all written into BROP
	2018.12	Hangzhou Branch of China Mobile, together with Hangzhou Municipal Government, built a "Direct Drinking Water System for Primary and Secondary Schools" project based on blockchain technology
	2019.1	Xihu District Procuratorate of Hangzhou Municipality and Ant Blockchain jointly developed and put into use the procuratorial blockchain forensics equipment, which combined the Internet of Things and blockchain technology, and could automatically generate forensics reports and carry out blockchain authentication on the integrity and authenticity of electronic data
	2019.3	Hangzhou Metro, together with Alipay, launched the electronic invoice based on blockchain technology
	2019.6	Hangzhou Internet Court launched the "5G + Blockchain" involving Internet implementation mode
Zhejiang	2019.4	Zhejiang Blockchain Notarization Lottery System began testing and officially started operation in May
	2019.6	The Blockchain Electronic Bill Platform initiated by Zhejiang Provincial Department of Finance was launched
Shanghai	2019.2	The People's Court of Pudong New Area in Shanghai adopted electronic evidences preserved by the judicial consortium blockchain IP360 as the basis for the trial
	2019.3	The Jing'an Sports Public Welfare Distribution platform of Jing'an District of Shanghai was officially launched

(continued)

Table 5.2 (continued)

Province/ city	Time	Content
Shenzhen	2018.8	The first blockchain electronic invoice in China was unveiled in Shenzhen. The blockchain electronic invoice was the first application research result of the "blockchain + invoice" ecosystem in China, which was governed by Shenzhen Taxation Bureau, and used the underlying technology provided by Tencent
	2018.9	The "Guangdong-Hong Kong-Macao Greater Bay Area Trade and Finance Blockchain Platform" was trial-run in Shenzhen
	2019.1	Shenzhen launched "iShenzhen" to build a blockchain electronic card platform through the blockchain
	2019.3	North Sea Fishing Village launched the blockchain electronic invoice product, solving the pain point of merchants in managing tax control equipment and computers. It was the first electronic invoice product generated by Shenzhen Taxation Bureau based on POS machine
Guangzhou	2017.10	WeBank, in conjunction with Guangzhou Arbitration Commission and Hangzhou YIBI Technology Co., Ltd., launched "Arbitration Chain" based on blockchain technology
	2018.2	Guangzhou Arbitration Commission issued the industry's first award based on the "Arbitration Chain"
	2018.6	Huangpu District of Guangzhou (Guangzhou Development Zone) Tax Bureau launched Guangzhou's first "Tax Chain" blockchain electronic invoice platform
	2018.10	Guangzhou Development Zone launched the "Policy Public Trust Chain"
	2019.3	Guangzhou Internet Court officially launched the "Online Law Chain" smart credit ecosystem
	2019.4	Huangpu District of Guangzhou launched a new commercial service blockchain platform. The platform integrated the existing policies of benefiting enterprises in Huangpu District and created a shared registration network based on the blockchain
	2019.6	Guangzhou Intermediate People's Court Smart Bankruptcy Trial System was launched, which was the first bankruptcy trial blockchain coordination platform in China
Guiyang	2017.5	Guiyang Hongyun Community joined hands with Wanglu Tech to build the blockchain poverty relief system of Hongyun Community so as to achieve targeted poverty alleviation and disability aiding through the blockchain platform
	2018.10	The blockchain intelligent public welfare platform set up by Guizhou Provincial Foundation for Poverty Alleviation was officially launched
	2019.1	Qingzhen City of Guiyang realized intelligent and digitalized rural grass-roots governance through blockchain technology
Qingdao	2019.6	Qingdao launched the "Government Knowledge Learning and Examination Platform" and the "Government KPI Assessment Platform" to streamline government affairs processes
	2019.7	Shibei District of Qingdao built an underlying data circulation network for government affairs and realized rapid data linkage and

(continued)

Table 5.2 (continued)

Province/city	Time	Content
		synchronization among government departments through the blockchain technology
Chongqing	2018.2	The Public Security Bureau of Chongqing Jiangbei District launched the "Community Police Intelligent Business Card" blockchain application project
	2018.6	Yuzhong District released the blockchain smart Party building information platform
	2018.11	A new government information resource sharing mechanism with blockchain technology as its core was established, and the application of blockchain technology to promote cross-level, cross-departmental and cross-regional sharing and mutual recognition of government materials such as electronic licenses was explored
	2019.1	The blockchain food and drug supervision and traceability platform was launched
	2019.6	The blockchain government service platform was launched
	2019.3	The newly registered business licenses in Chongqing Administration for Industry and Commerce were all included into the government blockchain
Foshan	2017.6	IMI Digital Identity Platform was officially launched. The platform relied on the blockchain to build intelligent multifunctional identity authentication
	2017.6	The blockchain governance platform was launched
	2018.11	Chancheng Government of Foshan launched the "Sharing Community APP", which was the latest practice of innovative "Blockchain + Sharing Community" grassroots governance in Chancheng
	2019.1	Chancheng District of Foshan planned to start the "Blockchain Pension Service" project and build a data sharing and linkage platform through blockchain technology so as to improve the service management mechanism
	2019.6	Chancheng District of Foshan launched the first "Blockchain + Vaccine" project in the province to build a "Blockchain + Vaccine Safety Management Platform". The whole process of vaccine circulation could realize visual supervision, thus making vaccines safer
Nanjing	2018.9	The Nanjing Arbitration Commission announced that it would launch the online arbitration platform which could realize real-time preservation of evidence, electronic delivery, online trial and adjudication by taking full advantage of blockchain technology and cooperating with certificate of deposit institutions, financial institutions, arbitration institutions, etc.

Source: China Academy of Information and Communication Technology, 2019 (*Blockchain White Paper (2019)*, China Academy of Information and Communication Technology, 2019-11-08)

characteristics as well as the actual landing scenarios so as to play a role in serving economic and social development.

Chapter 6
The Future of Blockchain

Blockchain is a data management technology, which is jointly maintained by multiple parties and uses cryptography to ensure the security of transmission and access, thus achieving data storage consistency and data tamper-proof. With its unique trust-building mechanism, the blockchain has realized penetrating prior supervision and trust step-by-step transfer, which is of great strategic significance to the construction of a new digital economic information infrastructure and the reshaping of the real economic development ecology.

The significance of blockchain can be understood from the perspectives of improvement and revolution. From the perspective of improvement, the blockchain helps to reduce costs and increase efficiency, and create new momentum for the development of the digital economy. Integrated with traditional modes of various industries, the blockchain is expected to release huge development potential. For example, in the field of government governance, the blockchain contributes to building a transparent and clean government and realizing smart government which means "data flows quickly for the convenience of the people". In the field of financial services, the blockchain technology is used to effectively solve the problems of "financing for small and micro enterprises being difficult and expensive", "optimizing the supply side" and "destocking", maintaining the stability of the capital chain and the high efficiency of capital flow of small and medium-sized enterprises in the supply chain, improving effectiveness and competitiveness of supply chain.

From the perspective of revolution, the blockchain affects the digital asset market and reshapes the financial and economic structure. The blockchain not only brings about technological improvements, but also further introduces new financial models and organizational forms, which involves core economic fields such as money creation and value circulation. For example, the Libra project initiated by Facebook aimed to build a global, decentralized, and programmable universal underlying financial infrastructure, which may have revolutionary significance to the current financial system.

Center for Electronics and Information Studies, Chinese Academy of Engineering, *The Development of Blockchain Technology*, https://doi.org/10.1007/978-981-16-7236-1_6

At present, the blockchain is mainly used to solve the trusted penetration of information flow among multiple subjects and open up the data silos. In the future, with the improvement of blockchain technology, application, and governance, the blockchain will become an important part of information infrastructure.

From the perspective of technology, the blockchain is still in the stage of rapid development, and various technological innovation schemes are emerging. In the future, further breakthroughs of the blockchain will be made in high-efficiency consensus protocols, blockchain performance optimization, interoperability technology, strongly constrained smart contract language, private computing technology and other aspects to further improve the technical scheme.

From the perspective of application, the application scenarios of blockchain technology continue to expand. From finance to coordination between digital identity and supply chain collaboration, the scenarios continue to deepen and diversify. On the one hand, the blockchain contributes to the real industry; on the other hand, it integrates traditional finance. The trust problems encountered during the blockchain optimizing the upgrading of traditional industries have greatly enhanced the upgrading of traditional industries, reshaped the trust relationship, and improved the efficiency of industrial coordination.

From the perspective of governance, the blockchain has continuously deepened the exploration of governance modes to form an industrial ecology with sustainable development and win-win results. As a technical scheme to reshape "production relations" and "trust relations", the implementation of blockchain application inevitably involves the rights and obligations among multiple subjects. The governance mode and development means forming more feasible and sustainable blockchain rules, and prescribing each member's role, voting weight, access mechanism, responsibilities, and benefit distribution, etc. These should be well integrated with the law to form a more efficient circle with trust and cooperation, and to give full play to the potential value of blockchain technology, thus becoming an important part of the information infrastructure in the digital age.

Printed in the United States
by Baker & Taylor Publisher Services